Thanksgiving Day Alphabet

Thanksgiving Day Alphabet

By
Beverly Barras Vidrine

Illustrated by
Alison Davis Lyne

PELICAN PUBLISHING COMPANY
Gretna 2006

For my grandchildren: Molly, Christopher, Courtney,
Bobby (deceased), Katie, Sydney, Ross, Kenneth, Addison. —B. B. V.

To history's pioneers, wherever they are. —A. D. L.

We acknowledge Carolyn Freeman Travers, research manager of Plimoth Plantation.

Text copyright © 2006
By Beverly Barras Vidrine

Illustrations copyright © 2006
By Alison Davis Lyne

The word "Pelican" and the depiction of a pelican are
trademarks of Pelican Publishing Company, Inc., and are
registered in the U.S. Patent and Trademark Office.

Library of Congress Cataloging-in-Publication Data

Vidrine, Beverly Barras.
  Thanksgiving Day alphabet / by Beverly Barras Vidrine ; illustrated by Alison Davis Lyne.
     p. cm.
  ISBN-13: 978-1-58980-338-1 (pbk. : alk. paper)
  1. Thanksgiving Day—History—Juvenile literature. 2. Alphabet books. I. Lyne, Alison Davis, ill. II. Title.
  GT4975.V53 2006
  394.2649—dc22

                              2006009786

Printed in Singapore
Published by Pelican Publishing Company, Inc.
1000 Burmaster Street, Gretna, Louisiana 70053

THANKSGIVING DAY ALPHABET

In the fall of 1621, English colonists in America, today known as Pilgrims, celebrated a harvest festival. They were joined by the Native Americans, who were members of the Wampanoag (WOM puh No ag) Nation. Two years later, the colonists observed a Thanksgiving holy day. They thanked God for the rain that helped their crops grow. As time passed, people combined the two celebrations and called it Thanksgiving Day. This holiday is a time when families give thanks to God for their blessings.

A is for America. About four hundred years ago, America was part of what was called the New World. Europeans saw this new country as a vast wilderness that offered people space to settle as well as more freedom.

B is for Bradford. William Bradford was the second governor of Plymouth Colony. He was thankful for its survival and for the good crops, so he called for a harvest celebration.

C is for colony. The colonists' settlement in the New World was called Plymouth Colony. They built their homes where the Wampanoag village of Patuxet (pa TUCKS et) once stood.

D is for deer. These animals roamed the land near Plymouth Colony and were hunted for food. The Wampanoag brought five deer to the 1621 harvest celebration.

E is for English colonists. This group of people from England left their country to live, work, and make a better life in America. The men, women, and children settled in a place now called Plymouth, Massachusetts.

F is for feast. The colonists and their Wampanoag guests shared many meals during the harvest celebration. They ate corn, wild turkey, and deer meat called venison.

G is for games. The colonists and the Wampanoag probably played sports during the harvest festival. Today, football games are an American Thanksgiving tradition.

H is for harvest. When the crops were gathered, the colonists rejoiced. There was enough corn for the celebration as well as for the coming months until the next harvest.

I is for Indians. Tribes of Native Americans were living in the New World when the colonists arrived. One of these tribes was the Wampanoag, who showed the colonists how to plant, hunt, and fish.

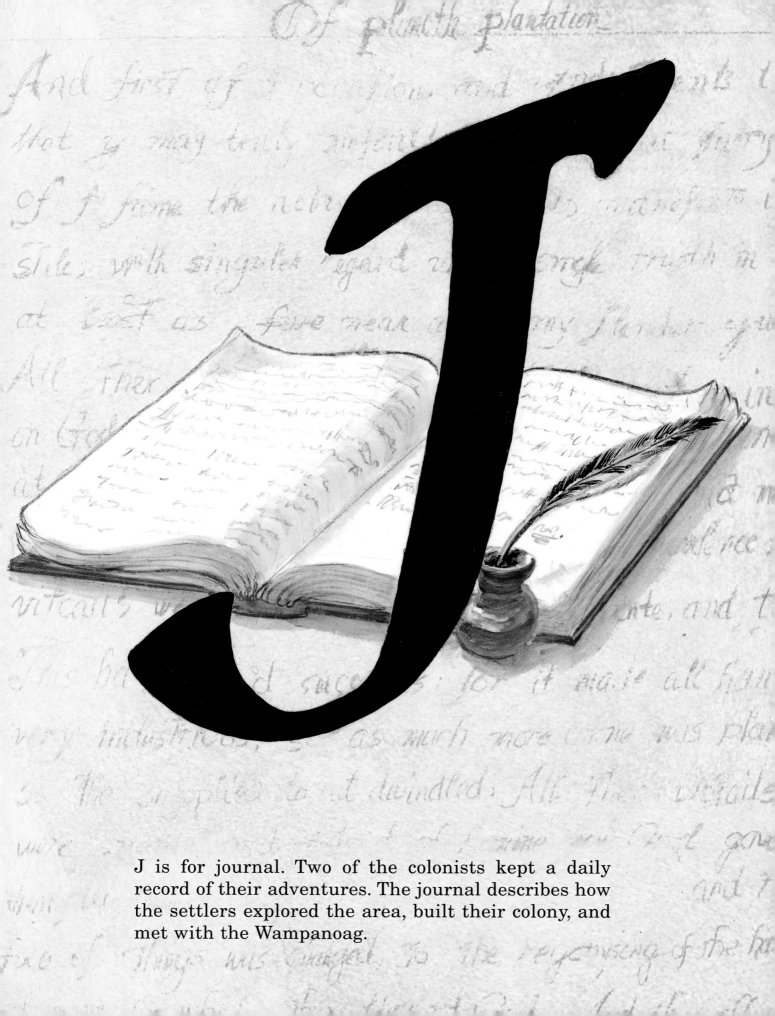

J is for journal. Two of the colonists kept a daily record of their adventures. The journal describes how the settlers explored the area, built their colony, and met with the Wampanoag.

K is for king of England. King James I was the head of the English church. When English people refused to attend his church, they were disobeying the king. Some of them left England so they could worship God in their own way.

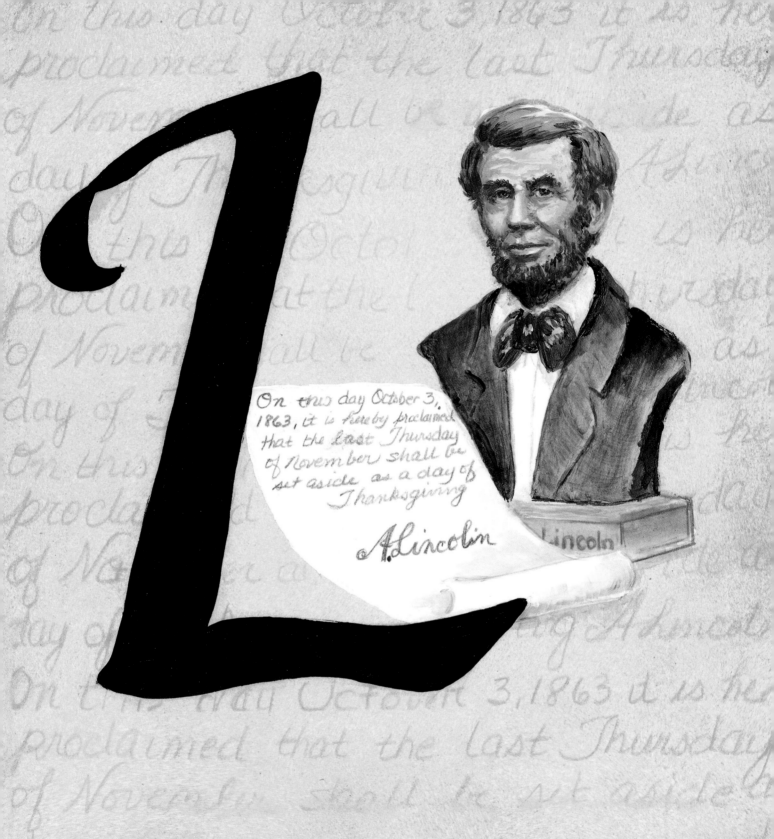

L is for Lincoln. Abraham Lincoln became president many years after the colonists landed in America. In 1863 he proclaimed Thanksgiving a national holiday.

M is for *Mayflower*. In 1620 the *Mayflower*, a small ship, sailed the Atlantic Ocean from England to America. The vessel carried 102 passengers and about twenty-five sailors.

N is for November. Thanksgiving Day is celebrated on the fourth Thursday of November every year. Also, the *Mayflower* reached America during this month in the year 1620.

O is for orange pumpkins. The round fruit grew on vines in the colonists' gardens and fields. The settlers sliced and cut the orange pumpkins then cooked them with spices.

P is for Pilgrims. A pilgrim is a person who travels for religious reasons. When the colonists from England left the English church, they went first to the Netherlands, and then they came to America. In time, all early Plymouth colonists became known as Pilgrims.

Q is for quill. The colonists wrote with pens made from goose or turkey feathers. They cleaned and trimmed the writing quill then dipped the pointed tip in ink to write.

R is for rules. The colonists agreed to stay together and obey the laws they made. They signed an agreement called the Mayflower Compact and elected John Carver as their first governor.

S is for Samoset and Squanto. The two Native Americans became friends with the colonists. They spoke the English language and helped the settlers survive in the New World.

T is for turkeys. Many turkeys wandered around the woodlands near the colony. The Wampanoag showed the colonists how to hunt these large birds for food.

U is for United States of America. Today, all the states in the U.S.A. celebrate Thanksgiving Day. A writer named Sarah Hale had the idea of celebrating the holiday all over America.

V is for voyage. The long journey across the ocean took about sixty-five days. Storms and rough seas shook the *Mayflower*. The passengers were crowded and cold, and many became seasick.

W is for Wampanoag. This tribe of people, who lived in America for many years before the *Mayflower* arrived, welcomed the colonists to the New World. Today, many Wampanoag still live in Massachusetts.

X is for X marks the spot. The letter X shows where the colonists settled and built homes. Their settlement was named New Plymouth after Plymouth, England, the city from which the colonists sailed for America.

Y is for Yellow Feather. Also known as Massasoit (MASS uh soyt), he was a chief of the Wampanoag tribe. He signed a treaty with the colonists, and he brought ninety men to the harvest celebration.

Z is for zea. This family of tall grass makes very big ears of corn. The colonists called it Indian corn because the Wampanoag people showed them how to plant it.